SCHOLAST

DISCO

Butterflies

Illustrated by Héliadore
Written by Gallimard Jeunesse
and Claude Delafosse

SCHOLASTIC REFERENCE
an imprint of
SCHOLASTIC

The butterfly
is an insect.

There are
500,000 species
of butterflies.
That's a lot of
butterflies!

The butterfly has six legs,
four wings, two antennae, and,
almost always, a tongue.

The tongue is like
a straw. It sucks up nectar.

The eyes have many sides
that can see movement
and color.

The butterfly uses its
two antennae to smell.

The butterfly's legs
are attached at the chest.
The butterfly uses its front
legs to taste sugar.

The butterfly's wing
has colorful scales.

Look up close
and see the scales!

Some butterflies are awake during the day....

Other butterflies are awake at night.

Butterflies eat nectar from flowers.

They fly from flower
to flower to eat nectar.

Pollen from a flower sticks to a butterfly's body. Then the pollen from one flower falls into another flower.

When a male and a female are ready to mate,
they perch on a stem.

Butterflies only mate with other
butterflies of the same species.

After carefully choosing a leaf,
the female butterfly lays her eggs.

When it's time to hatch,
the caterpillar larva breaks the egg with its jaws,
quickly eats the leaf around it, and grows until
it becomes an adult caterpillar.

Then the caterpillar stops
eating and becomes still.
Metamorphosis is about to begin.

The caterpillar hardens
into a chrysalis.
Inside, the caterpillar
is changing
into a butterfly!

The butterfly
splits open the
chrysalis and
climbs out.

Can you find the
butterfly that's hiding?
Turn the page....

The
camouflaged
butterfly
flies away!

To hide
themselves
from enemies,
some butterflies
camouflage
themselves,
or change
their colors,
to match a leaf
or some bark.

No-Brand
grass yellow

Hewitson's
blue hairstreak

Zebra
swallowtail

Tiger of Dalman

Queen Alexandra's
birdwing

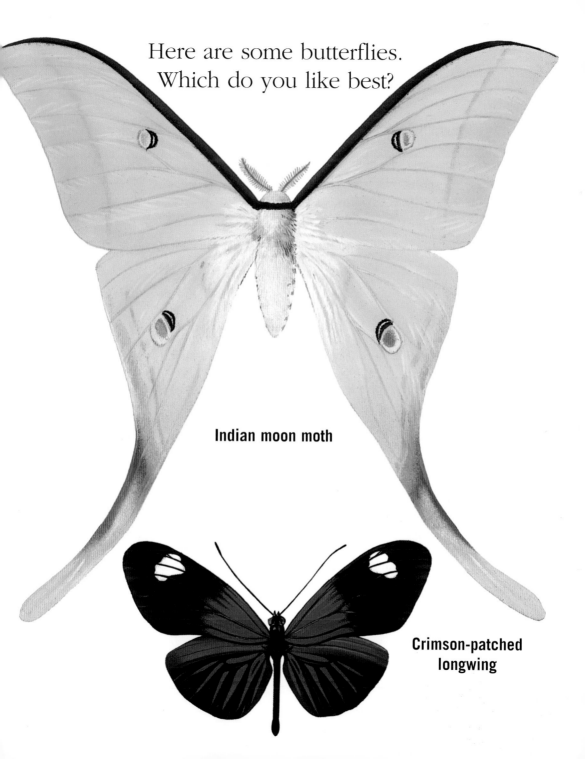

Here are some butterflies.
Which do you like best?

Indian moon moth

**Crimson-patched
longwing**

The **Western pygmy blue** is the world's smallest butterfly!

The **atlas moth** is found in India, Sri Lanka, China, Malaysia, and Indonesia. It has the greatest wing area of any butterfly.

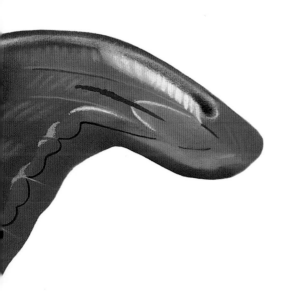

Here are some record-setting butterflies!

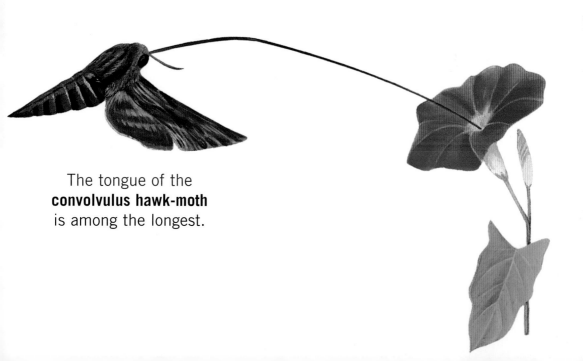

The tongue of the
convolvulus hawk-moth
is among the longest.

The larvae of some insects, such as the dragonfly, live in water.

Discover other metamorphoses.

Dragonfly

Ladybug

Cicada

The larvae of some insects
live aboveground,
while still others live
underground.

Death's head hawkmoth